POCKET POSITIVES
for
LIVING

POCKET POSITIVES *for*
LIVING
An Anthology of Quotations

Summit Press
950 Stud Road, Rowville
Victoria 3178
Australia

Email: publishing@fivemile.com.au
Website: www.fivemile.com.au

First published 2002 as *Pocket Positives for Our Times*
This revised edition first published 2006

This compilation © The Five Mile Press Pty Ltd

Compiled by Maggie Pinkney
Designed by Zoë Murphy
Illustration by Kieran Murphy
Printed in China

ISBN 1 74124 479X

CONTENTS

How to Be Happy

Getting in Touch with Your Creativity

What's it All About?

PREFACE

We have a choice about how we deal with life's endless challenges. We can react with hope or despair, with courage or fear, with enthusiasm or indifference.

This optimistic anthology comes down firmly on the side of the positive. Instead of focusing on life's difficulties, these inspirational quotations urge you to think of your many blessings, such as friends, family, and home. They also encourage you to believe in yourself, to set goals and to get in touch with your own creativity.

Poets, novelists, world leaders, and philosophers are among the many distinguished men and women whose reflections on life are included here. We can all learn from the combined wisdom of these beautiful minds.

Maggie Pinkney, 2006

HOLD ON TO HOPE

Hope is the power

of being cheerful in circumstances

that we know to be desperate.

———————

G. K. CHESTERTON, 1874–1936
English writer, poet and critic

We should never let our fears

hold us back

from pursuing hopes.

———————

JOHN F. KENNEDY, 1917–1963
President of the United States of America

The hope in the world
is still in dedicated minorities.
The trailblazers in human, academic,
scientific and religious freedom
have always been in the minority.

———————

MARTIN LUTHER KING JR., 1929–1968
American civil rights leader and minister

Do not fear to hope ... Each time

we smell the autumn's dying scent,

We know that primrose time

will come again.

———————

SAMUEL TAYLOR COLERIDGE, 1772–1834
English poet

True hope is swift and flies

with swallow's wings;

Kings it makes gods,

and meaner creatures kings.

WILLIAM SHAKESPEARE, 1564–1616
English playwright and poet

There is one thing

which gives radiance to everything.

It is the idea of something

around the corner.

———————

G. K. CHESTERTON, 1874–1936
English writer, poet and critic

There are no hopeless situations;

there are only men who have

grown hopeless about them.

CLARE BOOTH LUCE, 1903–1987
American playwright

Hold your head high,

stick your chest out.

You can make it.

It gets dark sometimes

but morning comes ...

Keep hope alive.

JESSE JACKSON, b. 1941
American minister, civil rights leader and congressman

Of all the forces

that make for a better world,

none is so indispensable,

none so powerful as hope.

Without hope man is only half alive.

———————

CHARLES SAWYER, 1887–1979
American lawyer

In future days,

which we seek to make more secure,

we look forward to a world founded upon four

essential freedoms. The first is the freedom of speech

and expression – everywhere in the world.

The second is freedom of every person to worship

God in his own way – everywhere in the world.

The third is freedom from want ...

the fourth is freedom from fear.

FRANKLIN D. ROOSEVELT, 1882–1945
President of the United States of America

We must accept finite disappointment,

but we must never lose infinite hope.

MARTIN LUTHER KING JR., 1929–1968
American civil rights leader and minister

Nothing worth doing

is completed in our lifetime;

therefore, we must be

saved by hope.

———————

REINHOLD NIEBUHR, 1892–1971
American theologian

For what human ill
does not dawn
seem to be an alleviation?

———————

THORNTON WILDER, 1887–1975
American dramatist and writer

Everything that is

done in the world

is done by hope.

_____

MARTIN LUTHER, 1483–1546
German religious reformer

Great hopes make great men.

THOMAS FULLER, 1608–1661
English clergyman and historian

MAKING IT HAPPEN

To will is to select a goal,

determine a course of action

that will bring one to that goal,

and then hold to that action

till the goal is reached.

The key is action.

———————

MICHAEL HANSEN, 1863–1908
American mathematician

If you will it, it is no dream.

THEODORE HERZL, 1860–1904
Zionist founding father

How wonderful it is

that nobody need wait a single

moment before starting to

improve the world.

———

ANNE FRANK, 1929–1945
German Jewish schoolgirl diarist

Just go out there and do what you have to do.

MARTINA NAVRATILOVA, b. 1956
Czechoslovakian-born American tennis champion

Action may not

always bring happiness,

but there is no happiness

without action.

BENJAMIN DISRAELI, 1804–1881
English statesman and writer

If one advances confidently

in the direction of his dreams,

and endeavors to live the life

which he had imagined,

he will meet with a success

unexpected in common hours.

———————

HENRY DAVID THOREAU, 1817–1862
American essayist and poet

The thing has already

taken form in my mind before I start it.

The first attempts are absolutely unbearable.

I say this because I want you to know that if you

see something worthwhile in what I am doing,

it is not by accident but because of

real direction and purpose.

VINCENT VAN GOGH, 1853–1890
Dutch post-impressionist painter

The first thing to do in life

is to do with purpose

what one proposes to do.

PABLO CASALS, 1876–1973
Spanish cellist, conductor and composer

Singleness of purpose

is one of the chief essentials

for success in life,

no matter what may be

one's aim.

JOHN D. ROCKEFELLER, 1874–1960
American oil millionaire and philanthropist

IT'S UP TO YOU

If you think you're a winner you'll win,

If you dare to step out you'll succeed.

Believe in your heart, have a purpose to start,

Aim to help fellow man in his need.

Thoughts of faith must replace every doubt,

Words of courage and you cannot fail.

If you stumble and fall, rise and stand ten feet tall,

You determine the course that you sail.

ANONYMOUS

The man who does things

makes mistakes,

but he never makes the

biggest mistake of all –

doing nothing.

BENJAMIN FRANKLIN, 1706–1790
American statesman and scientist

Look at your life as a beautiful
fabric woven from wonderful
rich colors and fine cloth.
Make a plan, one that is full of
obtainable goals for a happy life.
Read through the plan daily so that
it becomes a permanent part
of your thought process.

SARA HENDERSON, 1936–2001
Australian outback station manager and writer

All things are possible

until they are proved impossible –

and even the impossible may only be so,

as of now.

PEARL S. BUCK, 1892–1973
American writer and humanitarian

If you don't like the way the world is,

you change it.

You have an obligation to change it.

You just do it one step at a time.

MARIAN WRIGHT EDELMAN, b. 1937
American attorney and civil rights activist

Never look down to test the ground
before taking your next step;
only he who keeps his eye fixed on
the far horizon will find his right road.

DAG HAMMARSKJOLD, 1905 –1961
Swedish statesman and humanitarian

A SPECIAL KIND
OF COURAGE

We are all afraid –

for our confidence, for the future, for the world.

That is the nature of the human imagination.

Yet every man, every civilization,

has gone forward because of its engagement

with what it has set itself to do.

The personal commitment and the emotional

commitment of working together as one,

has made the Ascent of Man.

JACOB BRONOWSKI, 1908–1974
British mathematician, writer and TV presenter

Courage is
the price life exacts
for granting peace.

AMELIA EARHART, 1897–1937
American aviator

Never give in!

Never give in!

Never, never, never, never –

in nothing great or small,

large or petty – never give in

except to convictions of

honor and good sense.

WINSTON CHURCHILL, 1874–1965
British statesman and Prime Minister

My personal trials have also taught me

the value of unmerited suffering.

As my sufferings mounted I soon realized

that there were two ways

that I could respond to my situation:

either to react with bitterness

or to transform the suffering

into a creative force.

———————

MARTIN LUTHER KING JR., 1929–1968
American civil rights leader and minister

To endure is greater than to dare;

to tire out hostile fortune;

to be daunted by no difficulty;

to keep heart when all have lost it –

who can say this is not greatness?

WILLIAM MAKEPEACE THACKERAY, 1811–1863
English writer

Each time a man stands up for an ideal,

or acts to improve the lot of others, or strikes out

against injustice, he sends forth a tiny

ripple of hope ... those ripples build a current that

can sweep down the mightiest walls of oppression

and resistance.

ROBERT F. KENNEDY, 1925–1967
American lawyer and politician

Each person has inside a basic decency and goodness. If he listens to it and acts on it, he is giving a great deal of what it is the world needs most. It is not complicated but it takes courage. It takes courage for a person to listen to his own goodness and act on it.

PABLO CASALS, 1876–1973
Spanish cellist, conductor and composer

My message to you is:

Be courageous!

Be as brave as your fathers before you.

Have Faith!

Go forward.

THOMAS EDISON, 1847–1931
American inventor

It isn't for the moment you are struck that you need courage, but for the long uphill climb back to sanity and faith and security.

———————

ANNE MORROW LINDBERGH, 1906–2001
American pilot, poet and writer

We ourselves must pilgrims be,

Launch our Mayflower, and steer

Boldly on the desperate winter sea,

Nor attempt the Future's portal

With the Past's blood-rusted key.

JAMES RUSSELL LOWELL, 1819–1891
American poet, abolitionist and diplomat

He who has courage and faith

will never perish in misery!

ANNE FRANK, 1929–1945
German Jewish schoolgirl diarist

Be strong and of good courage:

be not afraid, neither be thou dismayed:

for the Lord thy God is with thee

whithersoever thou goest.

THE BIBLE, JOSHUA 1:9

Even under the most crushing
state machinery, courage rises up
again and again, for fear is not the
natural state of civilized man.

AUNG SAN SUU KYI, b. 1945
Burma's democratically elected leader

Courage is resistance to fear,

mastery of fear,

not absence of fear.

MARK TWAIN, 1835–1910
American writer

If suffering went out of life,

courage, tenderness, pity, faith,

patience and love in its divinity

would go out of life too.

FATHER ANDREW
Life and Letters

I would define true courage
to be a perfect sensibility
of the measure of danger,
and a mental willingness
to endure it.

GENERAL WILLIAM SHERMAN, 1820–1891
American military leader

'Tisn't life that matters!

'Tis the courage you bring to it.

SIR HUGH WALPOLE, 1884–1941
English writer

BELIEVE IN YOURSELF

Every individual human being born on this earth has the capacity to become a unique and special person, unlike any who has ever existed before or will ever exist again.

ELISABETH KÜBLER-ROSS, 1926–2004
American psychiatrist and writer

They are able who think they are able.

VIRGIL, 70–19 BC
Roman poet

I didn't belong as a kid,

and that always bothered me.

If only I'd known that one day

my differentness would be an asset,

then my early life would have been

much easier.

———————

BETTE MIDLER, b. 1945
American singer and comedian

Believe you can, and you can. Belief is one of the most powerful of all problem dissolvers. When you believe that a difficulty can be overcome, you are more than halfway to victory over it already.

———————

NORMAN VINCENT PEALE, 1898–1993
American writer and minister

Accept yourself as you are.

Otherwise you will never see opportunity.

You will not feel free to move toward it;

you will feel you are not deserving.

MAXWELL MALTZ, 1899–1975
American surgeon and motivational writer

I was raised to sense what someone else wanted me to be and to be that kind of person. It took me a long time not to judge myself through someone else's eyes.

SALLY FIELD, b. 1946
American actor

Care no more for the opinions of others,

for those voices.

Do the hardest thing on earth for you.

Act for yourself.

Face the truth.

———————

KATHERINE MANSFIELD, 1888–1923
New Zealand writer

Don't compromise yourself.

You are all you've got.

────────────

JANIS JOPLIN, 1943–1970
American singer and songwriter

Our problem is that we make the mistake of comparing ourselves with other people. You are not inferior or superior to any human being ... You do not determine your success by comparing yourself to others, rather you determine your success by comparing your accomplishments to your capabilities. You are 'number one' when you do the best you can with what you have, every day.

———————

ZIG SIGLAR
American motivational writer

In everyone there is something precious,

found in no one else; so honor each man

for what is hidden within him –

for what he alone has,

and none of his fellows.

HASIDIC SAYING

I'm trying to be myself more and more.

The more confidence you have in yourself ...

the more you realise that this is you,

and life isn't long. So get on with it!

————————

KYLIE MINOGUE, b. 1968
Australian singer and actor

Low self-esteem

is like driving through life

with your handbrake on.

MAXWELL MALTZ, 1899 –1975
American surgeon and motivational writer

Start treating yourself as if you're

the most important asset you'll ever have.

After all, aren't you?

——————

ANONYMOUS

He that respects himself
is safe from others.
He wears a coat of mail
that none can pierce.

——————

HENRY WADSWORTH LONGFELLOW, 1807–1882
American poet

Self-confidence

is the first requisite

of great undertakings.

———————

SAMUEL JOHNSON, 1709–1784
English lexicographer, critic and writer

THE HEART OF THE MATTER

To put the world in order we must first

put the nation in order.

To put the nation in order we must first

put the family in order.

To put the family in order we must first

cultivate our personal life.

And to cultivate our personal life,

we must set our hearts right.

———————

CONFUCIUS, c. 550–478 BC
Chinese philosopher

And now here is my secret,

a very simple secret; it is only with

the heart that one can see properly;

what is essential is invisible

to the eye.

ANTOINE DE SAINT-EXUPÉRY, 1900–1944
French novelist and aviator

The heart's affections are divided
like the branches of the cedar tree; if the tree loses
one strong branch, it will suffer but it does not die.
It will pour all its vitality into the next branch so
that it will grow and fill the empty space.

KAHLIL GIBRAN, 1882–1931
Lebanese poet, artist and mystic

Love will teach us all things,

but we must learn how to win love.

It is got with difficulty: it is a possession dearly

bought with much labor and a long time,

for one must love not sometimes only but always.

And let not men's sin dishearten thee:

love a man even in his sin, for that love is a

likeness of the divine love,

and is the summit of love on earth.

———

FEODOR DOSTOEVSKY, 1821–1881
Russian novelist

I love thee for a heart that's kind,

Not for the knowledge of thy mind.

———————

W. H. DAVIES, 1871–1940
Welsh poet

A loving heart is the truest wisdom.

———————

CHARLES DICKENS, 1812–1870
English novelist

If a good face

is a letter of recommendation,

a good heart

is a letter of credit.

———————————

EDWARD BULWER-LYTTON, 1803–1873
English writer, dramatist and poet

My heart is like a singing bird

Whose nest is in a watered shoot;

My heart is like an apple-tree

Whose boughs are bent with thickset fruit;

My heart is like a rainbow shell

That paddles in a halcyon sea;

My heart is gladder than all these

Because my love has come to me.

———————

CHRISTINA ROSSETTI, 1830–1894
English poet

Keep a green tree in your heart

and perhaps a singing bird

will come.

CHINESE PROVERB

All love is sweet,

Given or returned,

Common as light is love,

And its familiar voice

wearies not ever.

———————

PERCY BYSSHE SHELLEY, 1792–1822
English poet

The heart of the wise,
like a mirror,
should reflect all objects,
without being sullied by any.

CONFUCIUS, c. 550 – 478 BC
Chinese philosopher

Learning to understand our dreams

is a matter of learning to understand

our heart's language.

ANNE FARADAY, b. 1935
American psychologist and dream researcher

When thou prayest,

rather let thy heart be without words

than thy words without heart.

JOHN BUNYAN, 1628–1688
English writer and moralist

FAMILY TIES

From a letter to her mother

Whatever beauty or poetry is to be found in my

little book is owing to your interest and

encouragement of all my efforts from the first to

the last; and if ever I do anything to be proud of,

my greatest happiness will be that

I can thank you for that, as I may do for all the good

there is in me.

LOUISA MAY ALCOTT, 1832–1888
American novelist

My mother was the making of me. She was so true, so sure of me, and I felt that I had someone to live for; someone I must not disappoint.

THOMAS EDISON, 1847–1931
American inventor

I'm doing this for my father.

I'm quite happy that they see me as

my father's daughter. My only concern

is that I prove worthy of him.

———————

AUNG SAN SUU KYI, b. 1945
*Burma's democratically elected leader,
and daughter of Burma's hero Aung San*

To bring up a child

in the way he should go,

travel that way yourself

once in a while.

_____

JOSH BILLINGS, 1818–1885
American humorist

All that I am or hope to be,

I owe to my mother.

ABRAHAM LINCOLN, 1809–1865
President of the United States of America

By profession I am a soldier and take
great pride in that fact, but I am prouder,
infinitely prouder, to be a father.
A soldier destroys in order to build; the father
only builds, never destroys.
The one has the potentialities of death;
the other embodies creation and life.
And while the hordes of death are mighty,
the battalions of life are mightier still.

DOUGLAS MACARTHUR, 1889–1964
American military leader

There is no vocabulary

For the love within a family,

love that's lived in

But not looked at,

love within the light of which

All else is seen ...

———————

T.S. ELIOT, 1888–1965
American-born British poet and critic

If a child lives with approval,

He learns to like himself.

DOROTHY LAW NOLTE
American poet and writer

Children with the same family,

the same blood, with the same first

associations and habits, have some means of

enjoyment in their power, which no subsequent

connections can supply.

JANE AUSTEN, 1775–1816
English novelist

I long to put the experience of fifty years at once into your young lives, to give you at once the key of that treasure chamber every gem of which has cost me tears and struggles and prayers, but you must work for these inward treasures yourselves.

HARRIET BEECHER STOWE, 1811–1869
American author and abolitionist

YOUR CHILDREN

You may strive to be like them

but seek not to make them like you.

For life goes not backward

nor tarries with yesterday.

You are the bows from which your children

as living arrows are sent forth.

The Archer sets the mark

upon the path of the infinite,

And He bends you with His might that

His arrows may go swift and far.

Let your bending in the Archer's hand

be for gladness;

For even as He loves the arrow that flies,

so He loves the bow that is stable.

———————

KAHLIL GIBRAN, 1882–1931
Lebanese poet, artist and mystic

Family faces are magic mirrors.

Looking at people who belong to us,

we see the past, present and future.

GAIL LUMET BUCKLEY, b. 1937
American writer

I talk and talk and talk,

and I haven't taught people

in fifty years

what my father taught me by example

in one week.

———————

MARIO CUOMO, b. 1932
American politician

God sent children for another purpose than merely to keep up the race – to enlarge our hearts; and to make us unselfish and full of kindly sympathies and affections; to give our souls higher aims … and to bring around our firesides bright faces, happy smiles and loving, tender hearts.

MARY BOTHAM HOWITT, 1799–1888
English author

My mother had a great deal
of trouble with me,
but I think she enjoyed it.

MARK TWAIN, 1835–1910
American writer

I want my daughters to be beautiful,

accomplished, and good;

to be admired, loved and respected;

to have a happy youth,

to be well and wisely married,

and to lead useful, pleasant lives,

with as little care and sorrow to

try them as God sees fit to send.

LOUISA MAY ALCOTT, 1832–1888
American novelist

Love children especially for,

like angels, they too are sinless

and they live to soften and purify

our hearts and, as it were,

to guide us.

FEODOR DOSTOEVSKY, 1821–1881
Russian writer

There is no greater reward for a well-spent life than to see one's children well-started in life, owing to their parents' good health, good principles, fixed character, good breeding, and in general the whole outfit, that enables them to fight the battle of life with success.

WILLIAM GRAHAM SUMNER, 1840–1910
American sociologist

And so our mothers and grandmothers have, more often than not anonymously, handed on the creative spark, the seed of the flower they themselves never hoped to see – or like a sealed letter they could not plainly read.

ALICE WALKER, b. 1944
American writer

I think it must be written somewhere

that the virtues of the mother

will be visited on the children.

———————

CHARLES DICKENS, 1812–1870
English novelist

HOME, SWEET HOME

Home is any four walls
that enclose the right person.

HELEN ROWLAND, 1875–1950
American writer

He is happiest,

be he king or peasant,

who finds peace in his home.

JOHANN VON GOETHE, 1749–1832
German writer, dramatist and scientist

The ornament of the house

is the friends who frequent it.

———————

RALPH WALDO EMERSON, 1803–1882
American essayist and poet

A man travels the world over in search of what he needs and returns home to find it.

GEORGE MOORE, 1852–1933
Irish writer and art critic

The ideal of happiness has always

taken material form in the house

whether cottage or castle;

it stands for permanence and

separation from the world.

———————

SIMONE DE BEAUVOIR, 1908–1986
French novelist

No place is more delightful than one's own fireside.

CICERO, 106–43 BC
Roman orator, statesman and writer

Few things, including clothes,

are more personal than your cherished ornaments.

The pioneer women, who crossed a wild continent

clutching their treasures to them, knew that a clock,

a picture, a pair of candlesticks, meant home,

even in the wilderness.

———————

GOOD HOUSEKEEPING, AUGUST 1952

Seek home for rest,

For home is best.

———————————

THOMAS TUSSER, 1524–1580
English farmer

If you want one golden rule that
will fit everybody, this is it.
Have nothing in your houses that
you do not know to be useful
or believe to be beautiful.

WILLIAM MORRIS, 1834–1896
English designer and craftsman

But what on earth

is half so dear – so longed for –

as the hearth of home?

_____

EMILY BRONTË, 1818 –1848
English poet and novelist

Whom God loves,

his house is sweet to him.

MIGUEL DE CERVANTES, 1547–1616
Spanish writer

A comfortable home is

a great source of happiness.

It ranks immediately after health

and a good conscience.

———————

SYDNEY SMITH, 1771–1843
English essayist, clergyman and writer

My kitchen is a mystical place, a kind of temple for me. It is a place where the sounds and odors carry meaning that transfers from the past and bridges to the future.

———————

PEARL BAILEY, 1918–1986
American singer

The strength of a nation is derived

from the integrity of its homes.

———————

CONFUCIUS, c. 551–478 BC
Chinese philosopher

Mid pleasures and palaces

we may roam,

Be it ever so humble,

there's no place like home.

———————

J. H. PAYNE, 1791–1852
American dramatist, poet and actor

THANK HEAVENS
FOR FRIENDS

True happiness consists not in
the multitude of friends, but
in the worth and choice.

———————

BEN JONSON, c. 1573–1637
English dramatist and poet

You can always tell a real friend:

when you've made a fool

of yourself he doesn't feel

you've done a permanent job.

LAURENCE J. PETER, b. 1918
Canadian writer

The antidote for fifty enemies
is one friend.

ARISTOTLE, 384–322 BC
Greek philosopher

True friendship is a plant of slow growth

and must undergo and withstand

the shocks of adversity before it is

entitled to the appellation.

GEORGE WASHINGTON, 1732–1799
President of the United States of America

I always felt that the great high privilege,

relief and comfort of friendship was that

one had to explain nothing.

———————

KATHERINE MANSFIELD, 1888–1923
New Zealand writer

Love is like the wild rose-briar;

Friendship like the holly tree.

The holly is dark when the rose-briar blooms,

But which one blooms most constantly?

EMILY BRONTË, 1818–1848
English novelist and poet

I have learned that to have a good friend

is the purest of all God's gifts,

for it is a love that has no exchange

or payment.

—————————

FRANCES FARMER, 1910–1970
American actress and writer

The better part of one's life

consists of one's friendships.

ABRAHAM LINCOLN, 1809–1865
President of the United States of America

The proper office of a friend is to side with you when you are in the wrong. Nearly anybody will side with you when you are in the right.

MARK TWAIN, 1835–1910
American writer

It is one of the blessings of friends

that you can afford to be

stupid with them.

———————

RALPH WALDO EMERSON, 1803–1882
American essayist and poet

The world is a looking-glass,
and gives back to every man the
reflection of his own face.

WILLIAM MAKEPEACE THACKERAY, 1811–1863
British writer

You can make more friends in two months by becoming interested in other people than you can in two years by trying to get other people interested in you.

DALE CARNEGIE, 1888–1955
American motivational writer

Fate chooses your relations,

you choose your friends.

———————

JACQUES DELILLE, 1738–1813
French cleric and poet

The only way to have a friend is to be one.

RALPH WALDO EMERSON, 1803–1882
American essayist and poet

Friendship with oneself is all-important

because without it one cannot be friends

with anyone else in the world.

———————

ELEANOR ROOSEVELT, 1884–1962
First Lady of the United States of America

Friendship consists in forgetting

what one gives, and remembering

what one receives.

———————

ALEXANDRE DUMAS, 1803–1870
French novelist

If you want people to be glad to meet you,

you must be glad to meet them –

and show it.

JOHANN VON GOETHE, 1749–1832
German poet, writer and scientist

Friendship improves happiness and abates misery by doubling our joy and dividing our grief.

JOSEPH ADDISON, 1672–1719
English essayist

It is fit for serene days,
and graceful gifts and country rambles, but also for
rough roads and hard fare, shipwreck, poverty and
persecution ... It should never fall into something
usual and settled, but add rhyme and reason to what
was drudgery.

RALPH WALDO EMERSON, 1803–1882
American essayist and poet

It is a good thing to be rich,

and a good thing to be strong,

but it is a better thing to be

loved by many friends.

———————

EURIPIDES, c. 485–406 BC
Greek dramatist and poet

Friendship is the only cement
that will ever hold the world together.

———————————

WOODROW WILSON, 1856–1924
President of the United States of America

HOW TO BE HAPPY

I suspect that the happiest people you know

are the ones who work at being kind, helpful and

reliable – and happiness sneaks into their lives

while they are busy doing those things.

It is a by-product, never a primary goal.

HAROLD S. KUSHNER
American rabbi

He who wishes to secure the good of others has already secured his own.

CONFUCIUS, c. 550 – 478 BC
Chinese philosopher

There are as many nights as days, and the one is just as long as the other in the year's course. Even a happy life cannot be without a measure of darkness, and the word 'happy' would lose its meaning if it were not balanced by sadness.

CARL JUNG, 1875–1961
Swiss psychiatrist

The secret of happiness is this:

let your interests be as wide as possible,

and let your reactions to the things

and persons that interest you be

as far as possible friendly

rather than hostile.

BERTRAND RUSSELL, 1872–1970
English philosopher, mathematician and social reformer

Youth is happy because it has
the ability to see beauty.
Anyone who keeps the ability to
see beauty never grows old.

———————

FRANZ KAFKA, 1883–1924
Czechoslovakian-born German-speaking writer

I hope never to feel completely fulfilled because then the point of the journey would be destroyed.
You have got to have curiosity, hunger and slight anxiety.

JOANNA TROLLOPE, b. 1943
English novelist

Human felicity is produced
not so much by great pieces of
good fortune that seldom happen
as by little advantages that
occur every day.

BENJAMIN FRANKLIN, 1706–1790
American statesman, scientist and writer

There is a land of the living
and a land of the dead,
and the bridge is love.

THORNTON WILDER, 1897–1975
American dramatist and writer

A loving person lives in a loving world.

A hostile person lives in a hostile world.

Everyone you meet is your mirror.

───────────

KEN KEYES, JR, 1921–1995
Personal growth leader and peace advocate

Just don't give up trying to do

what you really want to do.

When there is love and inspiration,

I don't think you can go far wrong.

———————

ELLA FITZGERALD, 1918–1996
American singer

Live as if everything you do
will eventually be known.

HUGH PRATHER, b. 1938
American writer

In spite of illness, in spite even of
the arch-enemy sorrow, one can remain alive
long past the usual date of disintegration
if one is unafraid of change,
insatiable in intellectual curiosity,
interested in big things,
and happy in small ways.

———————

EDITH WHARTON, 1862–1937
American novelist

I accept life unconditionally.

Most people ask for happiness on condition.

Happiness can only be felt

if you don't set any condition.

ARTUR RUBINSTEIN, 1887–1982
Polish-born pianist

To find out what one is fitted to do

and to secure an opportunity to do it

is the key to happiness.

JOHN DEWEY, 1859–1952
American educationalist, philosopher and reformer

W hat can be added to the happiness of

a man who is in health, out of debt,

and has a clear conscience?

———————

ADAM SMITH, 1723–1790
Scottish economist, philosopher and essayist

GETTING IN TOUCH WITH YOUR CREATIVITY

Creativity is so delicate a flower

that praise tends to make it bloom,

while discouragement often nips it in the bud.

Any of us will put out more and better ideas

if our efforts are appreciated.

ALEX F. OSBORN, 1888–1966
American advertising director

When I am ... completely myself,

entirely alone ... or during the night when

I cannot sleep, it is on such occasions that

my ideas flow best and most abundantly.

When and how these come I know not,

nor can I force them.

———————

WOLFGANG AMADEUS MOZART, 1756–1791
Austrian musician and composer

Go cherish your soul;

expel companions;

set your habits to a life of solitude;

then will the faculties rise

fair and full within.

———————

RALPH WALDO EMERSON, 1803–1882
American essayist and poet

Emptiness is a symptom

that you are not living creatively.

You either have no goal that is

important enough to you, or you are

not using your talents and efforts

in striving toward an important goal.

MAXWELL MALTZ, 1899–1975
American surgeon and motivational writer

To me, the difference between
the artist and the non-artist
is that the artist is
the one that does it.

HELEN GARNER, b. 1945
Australian writer

When in doubt, make a fool of yourself.
There is a microscopically thin line between
being brilliantly creative and acting like
the most gigantic idiot on earth.
So what the hell, leap!

CYNTHIA HEIMEL
American writer

Don't think!

Thinking is the enemy of creativity.

It's self-conscious,

and anything self-conscious is lousy.

You can't try to do things;

you simply must do them.

RAY BRADBURY, b. 1920
American science fiction writer

A great many people who come

to creative writing classes intend

to write books 'one day'.

A book has to be written all the time,

it will not write itself one day.

A sense of dedication is necessary

to the writer.

———————

ELIZABETH JOLLEY, b. 1923
Australian writer

What is originality?

It is being one's self, and

reporting accurately what we see.

RALPH WALDO EMERSON, 1803–1882
American essayist and poet

No matter how old you get,

if you can keep the desire to be creative,

you're keeping the man-child alive.

JOHN CASSEVETES, 1929–1989
American film director

All you have to do

is close your eyes and

wait for the symbols.

TENNESSEE WILLIAMS, 1911–1983
American dramatist and writer

WHAT'S IT ALL ABOUT?

Be a good human being,

a warm-hearted affectionate person.

That is my fundamental belief.

Having a sense of caring, a feeling of compassion

will bring happiness or peace of mind to oneself

and automatically create a positive atmosphere.

DALAI LAMA, b. 1935
Tibetan spiritual leader

The ideals that have lighted my way and, time after time, have given me new courage to face life cheerfully have been Kindness, Beauty and Truth.

Life is not made up of
great sacrifices and duties
but of little things
in which smiles and kindness
given habitually are what
win and preserve the heart
and secure comfort.

———————

SIR HUMPHREY DAVY, 1778–1829
English chemist and inventor

The only interest in living
comes from believing in life,
from loving life and using all the
power of your intelligence
to know it better.

———————

EMILE ZOLA, 1840–1902
French writer

What is the use of living if not to
strive for noble causes and to make this
muddled world a better place for those
who will live in it after we are gone.

WINSTON CHURCHILL, 1874–1965
British Prime Minister

Life was meant to be lived.

Curiosity must be kept alive.

One must never, for whatever reason,

turn his back on life.

ELEANOR ROOSEVELT, 1884–1962
First Lady of the United States of America

The great essentials to
happiness in this life are
something to do,
something to love and
something to hope for.

JOSEPH ADDISON, 1672–1719
English essayist

Who will tell whether

one happy moment of love,

or the joy of breathing or walking on

a bright morning and smelling the fresh air,

is not worth all the suffering and effort

that life implies?

———————

ERIC FROMM, 1900–1980
American psychoanalyst

What do we live for,

if it is not to make life less difficult

for each other.

GEORGE ELIOT, 1819–1880
English novelist

Believe that life is worth living,

and your belief

will help create the fact.

_____

WILLIAM JAMES, 1842–1910
American psychologist and philosopher

Getting money

is not all a man's business;

to cultivate kindness is

a valuable part of the

business of life.

———————

SAMUEL JOHNSON, 1709–1784
English lexicographer, critic and writer

I expect to pass through life but once.

If, therefore, there be

any kindness I can show,

or any good thing I can do

to any fellow being,

let me do it now,

for I shall not pass

this way again.

WILLIAM PENN, 1644–1718
English Quaker and founder of Pennsylvania, USA

The root of the matter is a very simple

old-fashioned thing, a thing so simple that I am

almost ashamed to mention it for fear of

the derisive smile with which wise cynics

will greet my words.

The thing I mean – please forgive me for

mentioning it – is love, or compassion.

If you feel this,

you have a motive for existence,

a guide to action, a reason for courage,

an imperative necessity

for intellectual honesty.

———————

BERTRAND RUSSELL, 1872–1970
English philosopher, mathematician and social reformer